MW01240533

"Costa Rica: Bala

Communism, Revolutionaries & Paramilitaries, & the

Rising Threat from the Global Drug Trade"

James Korman

There is a question for which we will never know the answer: had the U.S. not launched the Contra war to overthrow the Sandinista government, would they have succeeded in bringing socioeconomic justice to the people of Nicaragua?

- Bianca Jagger

To my father whom I miss so dearly who passed away in March 2017 due to pancreatic cancer. I love you so much.

Table of Contents

The failure of US efforts & treaties in thwarting communism in the 20th century in Central America

A conference of Central American States met in Washington D.C. in 1922 pledging to seek foreign assistance in developing their armies with the hopes of establishing a more robust internal order. The U.S. uscd this opportunity to amplify its involvement in Central America as they feared the spread of Mexican Bolshevism during this time since Mexican Bolshevists continued to grant aid to Central American countries undermining the United States political and military strategy. However, in a change of heart, President Franklin D. Roosevelt in 1933 accepted the Convention on the Rights and Duties of States at the Montevideo Inter-American Conference. Thus, officially renouncing all United States meddling in Central American internal affairs. But when Harry Truman became President of the United States, the United States promoted the Rio Treaty (1947) and directly began to back any anticommunist government in Central America. Such backing and show of support for dictators like Somoza of Nicaragua tarnished America's image even more to many Central Americans. Costa Rica found this American support for Somoza gravely offensive as the Somoza regime in 1948 supported the government of Teodoro Picado against their revolutionary hero, Jose Figueres. The sentiment around

U.S. aid for the following three decades was a feeling that the U.S. was

solely promoting pro-Americanism and not pro-Communism – not

actually caring about the Central American nations and their interests.

U.S. assistance and aid in Latin America increased rapidly in 1959 with

the Cuban revolution. The Central American Defense Council

(CONDECA), which included all Central American nations but Costa

Rica was formed in 1961 with the purpose of equipping and training

militarily in coordination with the United States Southern Command to

counter Communist insurgencies. Moreover, the U.S. sponsored the

Alliance for Progress, reassuring developmentalism of Central

American countries by improving social and economic situations via

politically moderate methods. The Alliance increased aid to the region

with hopes of thwarting communist revolution. Around the same time,

the Central American Common Market was created with the goal of

increasing industrialization and diversification of export products

which lasted until roughly 1969. The Organization of American States

then had its turn operating throughout the 1970s that looked to improve

the quality of life in Central America. Through it all, the first

communist government in Central America captured power in

Nicaragua in 1979. A severe blow to the programs and alliances pushed by the United States as they had failed to stop the insurgency from taking power.[1]

The US—Costa Rica—Nicaragua trilemma

Border disputes with Panama and Nicaragua with Costa Rica were the prime sources of a U.S. response and Yankee involvement with the Costa Rican government during the early part of the 20th century. Elections also began during this time and Costa Rican governmental transformation was formed with very little United States intervention. However, trouble finally came Costa Rica's way in 1948 as the nation erupted into Civil War, led by Jose Figueres Ferrer who helped fight against government forces. This National Liberation War solidified Figueres a hero and friend of the United States as he also later ratified the Rio Treaty – a mutual defense pact with the inclusion of the United States as a friend to be leaned on to counter aggression. Almost immediately after, Nicaraguan ruler, Anastasio Somoza, sent troops to Costa Rica in what was a border war between the two nations. Figueres came out on top while also aiding the draft constitution in 1949 that still accounts for Costa Rican democracy today. Only in 1956 was a formal treaty of friendship between Costa Rica and Nicaragua finally signed, after another war with Nicaragua and the assassination of Somoza. This war with Nicaragua in 1955 elicited United states military aid to Costa Rica. Meanwhile, Nicaragua received assistance from Cuba, the Dominican Republic, Colombia, and Venezuela. As Somoza protested U.S. assistance including the sale of four P-51 fighter aircraft to Costa Rica for US $1 million apiece, the OAS condemned Nicaragua for its part in the invasion.[2]

Moving forward into the 1970s, Costa Rican relations with the United States became strained under the second Figueres Administration as Costa Rica established diplomatic ties with the Soviet Union a USSR embassy was opened in San Jose. Figueres had received campaign contributions from American financier Robert Vesco who was indicted by a U.S. court but fled to Costa Rica. The Costa Rican government protected this American from extradition.[3] At the same time that relations deteriorated with the United States, Costa Rica also began to experience a rising communist threat from communist agitators mainly from Nicaragua who had infiltrated Costa Rica in recent years. At first, Costa Rica aided the Sandinista communists against the corrupt and repressive Somoza regime in Nicaragua.[4] The United States was in part to blame as it left behind the National Guard in control of Anastasio Somoza Garcia whose family

reigned over Nicaragua for nearly 46 years after its earlier experiences
of empire in Nicaragua. The Somoza National Guard was Mafia like in
nature. But President Roosevelt desired to be a "good neighbor",
thereby eliciting a closer friendship with the autocratic regime. When
WW2 arose and the U.S. officially declared its entry, Nicaragua
quickly followed suit in declaring war against the axis powers. In the
1950s, the U.S. among other nations began to send more aid to
Nicaragua and soon, Somoza had the most powerful armed force in
Central America.[5] Furthermore, President Dwight D. Eisenhower
elicited the help of Somoza to help overthrow the Guatemalan
government in 1954 while Somoza continued to build his personal
fortune nearing $50 million while increasing the concentration of land
ownership in Nicaragua. When Somoza was finally killed in 1956 by
Rigoberto Lopez Perez, a young Nicaraguan poet, his brothers now
ruled Nicaragua and U.S. support for the regime only increased for the
following two decades. From 1953-1961, military aid centered around
$200,000 a year and jumping to roughly $1.8 million per year between
1967-1975. In total, between 1946-1975, U.S. military aid to Nicaragua
totaled $25.5 million. Unfortunately, Somoza used this aid to further
grow the corrupt family fortune to $300 million by 1972. Now, wealth
was heavily concentrated by the rich while Somoza continued to take

bribes for illegal gambling and prostitution while acquiring large coffee plantations and becoming the largest land owner and coffee producer in Nicaragua in its history. Moreover, To the detriment of the Nicaraguan people, an earthquake struck in 1972 in Managua killing more than ten thousand people. Somoza further transformed this national disaster into personal gain channeling international relief funds into his own piggy bank.[6] In the end, given this corruption perceived by Costa Rica on behalf of Somoza and the damage the regime did to the Nicaraguan people, it was only natural to lend a helping hand to the Sandinistas at first.

After years of corruption and deteriorating economic conditions, the Sandinista Front of National Liberation began to grow around 1973 and was named after Augusto Cesar Sandino. Nicaragua was clearly ready for change but the Nixon and Ford administrations continued to support Somoza as the FSLN continued to grow more powerful. But President Carter abruptly cut off aid to Nicaragua in 1977 due to human rights violations. More and more countries continued to support the rebel FSLN cause. For its part, Costa Rica permitted FSLN training bases and FSLN strikes against Nicaragua from Costa Rican soil as it borrowed weapons from Panama and

Venezuela to protect FSLN camps in the northern part of the country.
Costa Ricans even began enlisting in the FSLN and raising funds for
the rebels by 1978 culminating in the rupture of diplomatic channels
with Nicaragua. In 1979, Costa Rica permitted the FSLN to establish a
revolutionary government in exile while Honduras served as a
sanctuary for the FSLN. Moreover, Panama aided the rebels first hand
serving as an entry point for arms purchased from Cuba and other
countries by the FSLN. Somoza, angered, denounced Panama as a
communist puppet engaging in coup de tat like actions to overthrow
him. On top of it all, Mexico transformed into a center for rebel fund-
raising and coordination activities for the FSLN cause while rupturing
diplomatic ties with Nicaragua in May of 1979 while also pleading to
the OAS to oust the Somoza regime and provide international
recognition of the FSLN. Cuba for its part also played a key role in
providing aid to the FLSN from the 1960s until the end of Somoza's
rule in 1979.[7]

In another twist, the fear that Nicaragua might turn into
another Cuba was rationalized and due to this fear, Carter's
Administration decided to aid Somoza via the reversal of an earlier
policy that permitted a $66 million International Monetary Fund (IMF)

loan to Nicaragua for approval without US opposition. Carter also dogmatically commended Somoza in 1979 for the improvement of Nicaragua's human rights situation outraging many central American nations through this action while only gradually hurting Somoza's support. Incumbents and insurgents in Nicaragua took grave offense by U.S. actions at this time and by the end of the 1980's, Nicaragua was more than $1.5 billion in debts while the Marxists were now in power and U.S. relations became severely strained.[8]

Costa Rica for its part also flipped on its support for the FSLN cause as the new Sandinista government in Nicaragua in 1979 was accused of leading strikes in the banana plantations – one of Costa Rica's biggest industries. Furthermore, in May of 1981, Costa Rica severed relations with Cuba preceding the election of Luis Alberto Monge Alvarez in 1982 with his administration set to receive much larger amounts of United States security assistance to counter the communist threat. The United States remained the sole supplier for military aid to Costa Rica in the 1980s. It increased from $0 in 1981, to $1 million in 1982, up to $4.6 million by 1983 and nearly $9.2 million in 1984, culminating in nearly $11 million in 1985.[9]

**Transregional events of the 1980s impeding US efforts at thwarting
communism and the Sandinistas**

After the Sandinista Revolution, relations were severely
hampered with the United States and Central American countries.
Nicaraguan exports to the United States diminished from $150 million
in 1978 to $96.5 million in 1982. In total, since the revolution, $250
million worth of export revenue loss surmounted to more than $400
million by 1982. In the same year, 80 percent of Nicaragua's export
income was either financing the national debt or paying for petroleum
imports. Severe shortages of food and medicine were still prevalent in
Nicaragua while the revolutionary government continued to place the
blame on the United States for its economic nationalism in cutting of
aid, loans, and eliminating trade with the communist Sandinistas.[10]
Hostility toward the Nicaraguan government on behalf of the Reagan
administration stemmed from fallacious ideology and viewpoints. His
administration described Nicaragua as a "totalitarian dungeon". Yet,
Nicaragua did not impose a one-party state nor nationalize any of the
country's productive property let alone suspend civic and human rights
initiatives. The Nicaraguan government at the time even adopted a new
constitution that called for open and competitive elections in 1985, and

moved them to 1984 to meet US demands. The Sandinista regime also posed a negligible threat to the US. However, the Sandinista regime did state that it would never permit foreign military bases on its territory.[11] Thus, making Costa Rica a crucial player in this high stakes Cold War game.

Meanwhile, Panama had its first national election for the first time in 16 years in May 1984. However, in September 1985, little under a year in office, Panamanian President Barletta was forced to resign by Panamanian strongman, General Manuel Antonio Noriega, leader of the country's military. Now, Panama was ruled by a corrupt military dictatorship but any United States action against Noriega could prove counter-productive via exacerbating already traditional Panamanian anti-Americanism as many Panamanians resent United States involvement in their domestic problems. This posed a challenge for the Reagan Administration which had to balance the assurance of United States national interests in the region while managing the corrupt Panamanian regime.[12] Still, The U.S. had one sole ally in the region as Reagan cherished Costa Rica's democracy entailing U.S. support for the country will endure both economically and with its domestic security.[13]

Conflicting Interests

On September 25, 1986 Costa Rican officials held a press conference to disclose a secret airstrip at Santa Elena that had been used for resupply for the Contras and for drug trafficking.[14] This declassified intelligence from the Digital National Security Archive is pivotal in explaining the conflicting interests of the United States and its Central American partner, Costa Rica, along with Mexico and other countries in the Central American region. Countries of which historically defied the U.S. in the face of overwhelming political and economic pressure during this period in the mid-1980s. Thus, exacerbating an already difficult situation for Costa Rica as Costa Rican officials sought to ally with the United States to isolate Nicaragua and allow Contra groups to use Costa Rican territory while others wanted to remain neutral while dealing with Costa Rica's economic problems.[15]

It was clear the United States was not going to let up on its efforts to secure a US friendly Central American region either. Economic problems of Costa Rica at the time can be attributed to Marxist politics. Such politics make foreign capital hesitant as they breed uncertainty and distrust for private enterprise. Lack of sufficient security assistance to safeguard economic growth thwarted any attempts at economic growth. Moreover, in 1984, the National Bipartisan Commission on Central America in 1984 concluded that Central America is vital and vulnerable and the US must not turn its head away from the region.[16] The Commission headed by Henry Kissinger was explicit that further Marxist-Leninist insurgencies will exacerbate deterioration and aid Soviet and Cuban power in the region. Thus, entailing the need for the US to defend against security threats near its borders. Aside from security implications, economic implications were pivotal. More than half of other foreign cargo, including crude oil was shipped to the United States through this Central American transit in the 1980s. The commission further recommended that Panama must not be threatened since a threat to the Canal automatically serves as a strategic threat to the United States. The report also found that Soviet use of Nicaragua as a base for expansionism was a principal threat to the security interests of the United States.[17]

The Soviet Union and United States avoided the folly of direct military conflict as they competed against each other in a strategic stalemate setting and waged their war on the third world. The U.S.

adapted its security policies of a containment doctrine and every corner

of the world was of potential strategic interest. It didn't matter the

political ideology of the regime. Even moderate to conservative

regimes that sought to promote their own national interests were

constrained by omnipotent US influence as they came under assault

from Washington. In turn, collaboration with the United States often

entailed ignoring or suppressing one's own local interests while

erecting governance that favored US policies.[18] The issue of why Latin

American countries pursued efforts that directly countered the

hegemonic United States is thus, a question of many. These policies

were risky as one takes into account holistically the Reagan

Administration's stronghold for a military strategy. The Reagan

administration was bent on defining the Central American crisis as an

East-West conflict and arena for U.S.-Soviet competition. The

designers of peace plans blatantly rejected the Reagan Administration's

efforts at solving the crisis militarily.[19]

As the Reagan Administration viewed Central America as a

principal theater of the Cold War – leftist elements in El Salvador,

Guatemala, and Nicaragua epitomized the struggle against Soviet

communism. Therefore, one would expect the United States to exert significant pressure on Mexico and Costa Rica to obtain their cooperation in the campaign to exterminate the leftist threat. Especially given the Reagan Administration's policy of linking U.S. aid benefits to compliant foreign policy behavior.[20] The core is able to exert significant pressure on the peripheries economic dependence. The United States had and still does maintain extreme policy leverage over Mexico and Costa Rica. Given that these two countries are inherently dependent on the United States for their economic survival made their anti-U.S. foreign policies even more intriguing.[21]

The global recession of the 1980s severely impacted both Costa Rica and Mexico domestically economically. Severe liquidity problems in the respective national treasury of each country resulted due to growing external debt and shrinking world export markets. Economic assistance by both the Madrid and Arias governments alleviated economic woes to some extent but it intensified already dependent ties.[22] Unemployment more than doubled between 1980-1982 in Costa Rica while national per capita income dropped 18 percent. In part due to the decline in coffee prices accompanied by rising oil prices – forcing Costa Rica to borrow heavily from the international community.[23] Their foreign debt stood at over $4 billion in 1985 while interest payments in 1983 were valued at $500 million. For Costa Rica, the economic difficulties for the Arias Administration were centered on foreign debt. Costa Rica's debt level was more than $4 billion in 1986 and negotiations splintered between Costa Rica, the IMF, and the World Bank as Costa Rica could not meet the proposed deficit spending targets. The World Bank mandated that Costa Rica reduce import tariffs cutting the $21.8 million deficit of the Consejo Nacional de Produccion (CNP), Costa Rica's price making agency for grains. The deficit arose due to price subsidies for rice, beans and maize. Further hindering Costa Rica economically was a US $30 million loan delayed until the World Bank released its funds. President Arias wanted to keep Costa Rica a welfare state not a garrison state. Raising concerns on behalf of the Reagan Administration concerning the new President's priorities given that Arias also stated if he were in Reagan's place, the allocation of US $100 million Contra aid would go to development programs instead.[24] Costa Rica was not going to budge on public expenditure spending as it is accustomed to devoting a large proportion of its annual budget towards education and social welfare programs. With the IMF and World Bank historically reluctant to tolerate "welfare" spending of debt-ridden countries, U.S. assistance was able to ease the harmful impacts of Arias's debt management on the local economy as the 1986 debt renegotiation granted Costa Rica the ability to spend 40% of its foreign exchange to service the debt rather than the expected 50% to 60%. If the U.S. didn't pressure Costa Rica's creditors to give the nation "special treatment" to its regional ally – these terms would not have come to fruition.[25] Moreover, direct bilateral aid between Costa Rica and the United States also contributed to improving Costa Rica's balance of payments. USAID granted $80 million in economic support funds to Costa Rica in 1986. Meanwhile, U.S. aid more than quadrupled between 1981 and 1986 and was key to Costa Rica's managed economic recovery. A sharp decline in U.S. assistance would have led to Costa Rican economic collapse.[26] Yet, it's important to note that the huge debt could pose a problem for the US banking system and international financial system as perceived at the time – thus requiring United States assistance, willingly or unwillingly.[27]

Costa Rica relied on U.S. markets as Costa Rican trade with its Central American neighbors declined from $187 million in 1985 to $99 million in 1986 – increasing Costa Rica's reliance on extra regional trading partners – including the United States.[28] Moreover, the United States continual ability to achieve its goals in the region even amidst the face of policy opposition by many Latin American leaders was evident by the Latin American debtor's association never being able to present a unified coalition for proposals to the debt crisis. This demonstrated Washington's continued influence in choosing the strategies it wants to pursue and achieve.[29]

Finally, although ubicated in a highly militarized region, Costa Rica maintains no standing army and the Rio Treaty protects Costa Rican national integrity in theory. However, the Rio Treaty has had a poor track record in preventing regional conflict making it an unreliable mechanism for ensuring Costa Rican security. This signifies that its national defense capabilities lie largely within other countries' perceptions of its alliance with the United States. Growing regional hostilities require these perceptions to persevere. The historical tensions between Nicaragua and Costa Rica – in light of the Sandinista arms build-up, made Costa Ricans truly concerned that conflict with Nicaragua would reoccur.[30] This also allowed the United States to nudge itself into the internal affairs of the tiny Central American nation.

The Peace Process relating to the Contra War

Central America served as a liberal peace-building paradigm laboratory for the rest of the world.[31] Dealing with proxies was an inherent component of reaching lasting peace in the region. Proxy arrangements for fighting were widespread but only came to vivid light through the Iran-Contra affair where scholars were able to study the impact of proxies in detail.[32] Proxy networks are forged in secrecy and with minimal (if any) consultation with Congress and are not formal alliance structures. American dependence on overseas proxies has thus generated a plethora of international commitments from supplying military and economic assistance to performing political and diplomatic favors. Even as extensive as providing aid for the survival of particular regimes.[33] US sanctioned Contra proxies contributed to the lack of social and economic mobility accompanied by the high levels of poverty contributed to the illegal immigration to the United States and Costa Rica (in Nicaragua's case).[34]

The exclusion of the United States from direct participation in the peace process communicated to U.S. policymakers that the U.S. had lost its hegemonic right to determine unilaterally hemispheric events.[35] The peace plans placed high priority on the elimination of external military support for Central American insurgency movements leading to an outright rejection of the Contra presence directly countering a major element of the Reagan Doctrine—armed support for anti-

Communist groups. However, U.S. support for the Contras continued unwaveringly despite the adoption of both Contadora and Esquipulas II. The call for Contra elimination directly challenged the Reagan Administration at the heart of its Central American policy.[36] The 1983 meeting on the island of Contadora on behalf of Colombia, Mexico, Panama, and Venezuela to architect a peaceful solution to the disputes erected in a 21-point peace plan called the "Document of Objectives". This document entailed the establishment of democratic systems of governance; reducing arms inventories and military personnel; eliminating foreign military bases and advisors; the end of support for subversive activities; and adequate methods of verification for these proposed objectives. Initially, Nicaragua was a signatory to the treaty on September 9, 1983 but on the 20th of October, 1983, four draft treaties were presented to the United Nations disregarding the objective of restoring military balance among states of the region while ignoring the Contadora objective of the establishment of democratic modes of governance effectively nulling the peace plan.[37] Deteriorating relations with the U.S. continued in 1984 as Nicaragua shot down a U.S. helicopter on the Honduran border zone in January while Nicaraguan accusations in March 1984 accused the CIA and U.S. government of mining ports along its Atlantic coast leading Nicaragua to litigate the

U.S. in the International Court of Justice and a win for Nicaragua as the ICJ ruled in its favor. This action significantly augmented the U.S. Congress's decisions to halt further aid to the Contras in 1984.[38]

Eventually all negotiations were then unilaterally ruptured with the United States in January 1985. On March 22, 1986, Contra forces in Honduras were attacked armed by Soviet, Cuban, Libyan, Iranian, North Korean, and Czech weaponry with the help of more than $500 million in military assistance from the USSR since 1980. Interestingly enough, Libyan leader at the time and now deposed and dead dictator, Moammar Khadafy, also sent $400 million in weapons and advisors to Nicaragua. President Reagan said that Khadafy was aiding Nicaraguans because they fight the U.S. on its own ground. But the well-armed Nicaraguan force was pushed back by the U.S. backed Honduran forces especially when the Reagan administration granted $20 million in emergency military aid for Honduras on March 24, 1986 facilitating the defeat of the Sandinistas. [39] President Reagan was explicit in U.S. interests of containing Nicaragua so it did not hurt its neighbors through the export of subversion and violence. President Reagan also viewed the sea lanes of Central America and the Caribbean Sea as vital to U.S. interests comparing the Soviet threat in the

Caribbean to Nazi activity in the region during WW2 adding that President Reagan carried a strong sentiment that all of the national security of America is at risk due to the ongoing crisis in Central America.[40] Meanwhile, Reagan's gem, Costa Rica, continued to be trapped between the corrupt military dictatorship of Panama and the Communists in Nicaragua.[41]

As Oscar Arias assumed the Costa Rican Presidency in 1986, an even greater communist threat was presenting itself. Further hurting the situation for Costa Rica was the fact that the tiny Central American nation became saturated with Nicaraguan and Cuban refugees. More than 250,000 Nicaraguans made their new home in Costa Rica. Meanwhile, the policy of the Arias Administration for the refugees was to deport only the ones in Costa Rica for economic reasons rather than political reasons. The United States at the present time aided the Arias administration with the reinforcement of military engineers to Costa Rica for highway improvements along with increased security assistance.[42]

Meanwhile, the Contras had already launched an estimated 163 attacks from Costa Rica against Nicaragua.[43]Therefore, the U.S., fearful of Costa Rican and Mexican inadequate police plans, aggressively lobbied and pressured its closest Central American allies (Costa Rica, El Salvador, and Honduras) to insist on modifications in the treaty that they knew all along would be unacceptable to Nicaragua. Evident by the faltered negotiations and the treaty went unsigned.[44] The Contadora peace went unsigned according to Bishop because the Sandinistas would only sign in it if the U.S. stopped all support for the Contras. Ideas at peace were further discussed at a Central American Presidents' meeting at Esquipulas in June with the hopes of creating a Central American Parliament or reactivating the Central American Defense Council. Still, no solution would be possible without US assistance but it was clear that the Central American countries desired more control of their problems and futures.[45]

Nonetheless, Arias achieved success that culminated in the signing of the Central American Peace Accords. El Salvador and Honduras joined the accords even amongst continued pressure by the U.S. not too. The treaty went into effect August 7, 1987. What helped the process significantly was that all five presidents in the Central American region shared a common desire to reach an agreement outside of U.S. influence. Even though in subsequent meetings, the Central American leaders could not converge on a final implementation leaving the peace process incomplete – the Arias Peace Plan still provided members of the U.S. Congress with reason not to fund the Contras.[46] Later, Special Assistant for National Security Affairs, General Colin Powell, was sent by the Reagan Administration to the capitals of El Salvador, Honduras, and Costa Rica to advise these participants to abandon the peace process If Nicaragua fails to democratize fully. Threats were made vehemently that the United States would "lose interest" in Central America – implying the loss of economic and military aid. Honduras and El Salvador ceded to U.S. demands and refused to agree on the details needed to adopt the peace plan. Only President Arias of Costa Rica stood firm in his resolve.[47]

Flirting with drug trafficking, proxies, the CIA and capitalist might

The closest neighbors of the United States in Latin America adopting Communism despite the fact that their populations are by and large filled with devout Christians is indeed a good question. Communism is atheist in nature. The only way that the doctrines of Communism and Christianity can be combined is rampant poverty. It is a fact that countries with a large disillusioned, poor class are prime countries for Communism. It's easy to sway the ideology and opinion of these people as Communism spreads social equity, employment for all, free education, and free medication.[48]

The Iran-Iraq War served as a precursor to the Iran-Contra affair. The freeing of US hostages held by pro-Iranian factions in Lebanon lured the US to sell arms to Iran on behalf of the Reagan administration. This funding allowed the continued arming of the anti-Sandinista Contras.[49] Meanwhile, the numerous numbers of unmonitored small airstrips near the Nicaraguan border on Costa Rican soil represented a critical supply route for the Sandinistas during the anti-Somoza insurgency. After this effort was succeeded in 1979, the surplus of weapons originally stored for use by the Sandinistas were then sold on the regional black market. Upon the establishment of the Southern Contra Front in 1983, Costa Rica was still ill-equipped to deal with other threats aside from the Contra war. Principally, those threats posed by the Colombian drug cartels of which started to ship cocaine through the Central American corridor as the Miami corridor was increasingly coming under intense surveillance.[50] Allegations in the media and congressional hearings that a significant amount of drugs, money, and arms, moved through Costa Rica had been pervasive complicating the socio-political situation. These allegations had been furnished by hearings before the U.S. Senate Subcommittee on Terrorism, Narcotics and International Communications of the Committee on Foreign Relations who heard evidence from a multitude of witnesses claiming an existing connection between C.I.A. covert operations, the Contras, drug flows, guns, and money into and out of the northern region of Costa Rica. The Costa Rican Press had corroborated some of these stories.[51]

Costa Rica lacked its own military and had limited law enforcement resources with subpar radar system capabilities.[52] But Many of Costa Rica's officers in its police force had attended United States military training programs erecting a closer relationship between the United States military and a multitude of Costa Rican officers as the U.S. operated a special Defense Agency within Costa Rica supporting Costa Rica's new defense capabilities.[53]

But U.S. militarization of Costa Rica's police forces wasn't enough to stop the Contra supply aircraft from utilizing these airstrips with impunity. This now meant that both Colombian and Panamanian drug operatives were well positioned to exploit the infrastructure that served the Southern Contra Front. The infrastructure became increasingly more crucial to traffickers as the early 1980s were a period when the cocaine trade to the U.S. from Latin America experienced exponential growth. It was thus confirmed that Contra operations on the Southern Front were funded by drug operations. Furthermore, weapons procured for the Contras were shipped from Panama on small planes that contained mixed loads of both arms and drugs. The pilots in the drug trade would often unload the weapons for the Contras at these various airstrips in Costa Rica.[54] Then, the trafficker pilots would refuel and fly north toward the U.S. with their drug cargo. Principally, the traffickers looked to shift their enterprise and distributional networks to the part where the highest added value can be added to the drug product – its movement into the United States via the US-Mexico border.[55] The pilots were American, Panamanian, and Colombian and some were even uniformed members of the Panamanian Defense Forces. Once this route was firmly established – it was an inevitable route to be used to refuel for traffickers, even if there were no weapons to be unloaded to arm and equip the Contras.[56] Facilitating this clandestine drug trafficking came with greater ease if one undertook vowed anti-communist rhetoric which came with the granting of additional military aid elevating officers in Honduras, El Salvador, & Panama to positions in which their roles allowed for the facilitation of drug trafficking via airstrips while the left leaning countries of Cuba, El Salvador and

Colombia were also implicit in drug trafficking. Although no evidence

of such events were found in Costa Rica, the constant references to

Costa Rica in the Senate Hearings on Drugs and Terrorism paint the

picture that the narcotics trade was vibrant in Costa Rica but its

direction and impact remained unclear. Numerous sources suggested

that the great value of money made available through Narco dollars

created a threat of subversion to all countries including the United

States.[57]

It was clear that a stronger force was winning while turning a

blind eye to this illicit drug trade: the market (with the added advent of

US complicity).[58] In shifting to South America, the region accounted

for nearly 90% of the cocaine that hit the U.S. markets in the mid-

1980s. The realization to many Latin American countries that drugs

were not the only problem came at the expense of the campesinos who

continued to grow drugs in order to hedge against their country's low

incomes, pervasive poverty, and high unemployment. This burgeoning

narcotics trade on behalf of small-time campesinos erected linkages to

insurgents who protected the production and transportation of drugs in

return for arms and supplies with the intent of further destabilizing the

economy. The dilemma became evident – drug eradication expounded the alienation of many Latin American countries populations while drug production augmented insurgent destabilization of the country.[59] Meanwhile, aircraft using the strips in Central America were immune from serious searches while US involvement and complicity rendered the traffickers "protected". Ultimately, the interchangeability of the infrastructure used by the Contras and the drug traffickers was explicit.[60]

Historical conflicts with Nicaragua and the lack of democracy in Central America gave more concern to Arias than threats of foreign military intervention. The Nicaraguan revolution did not end political stress between Nicaragua and Costa Rica. The 1987 revelation that an airstrip in Costa Rica was used to supply the Contras magnified existing tensions between the two. Arias was weary of Nicaraguan communist ties and preferred a more friendly, democratic nation as its neighbor. As Arias saw it, democratization was needed to bring the region out of bloodbath. As long as the wars continued, El Salvador, Honduras, Guatemala, and Nicaragua had little incentive to strengthen their democratic processes. This led to more economic devastation and domestic opposition while encouraging foreign military intervention.[61] At the same time, the state's capacities to offer employment in the formal sector which is needed for the integration of ex-combatants, migrants, and displaced people was stifled by neoliberal economic policies. Traditional elites and conflict entrepreneurs were those who gained the most from the privatization of state enterprises.[62]

In culmination, U.S. pressure on Costa Rica to change up its Central America policy was more forthright. Its massive displeasure with Arias's regime closing the airstrip at Santa Elena that supplied U.S. covert operations was evident by the U.S. government unofficially withholding $80 million in balance-of-payments assistance during the 1987 fiscal year. Frank McNeil, the former U.S. ambassador to Costa Rica even testified to the House Foreign Affairs Subcommittee on Inter-American Relations that Costa Rica received "less favored nation" status due to its independent decision making towards providing a solution to the Central American conflict.[63]

US complicity & complacency – the deceitfulness of the Reagan Administration

Jorge Morales, a top Colombian smuggler based in Miami who was already indicted for drug smuggling sought an alliance with the Contras in the hopes of using their CIA contacts to aid him in the charges brought against him. A U.S. State Department report indicated in late 1984 that Morales supplied C-47 aircraft and money to fly narcotics shipments from South America into Costa Rica and Nicaragua for eventual transport into the United States. 24 flights between October 1984 and February 1986 were carried out southward from the United States to Southern Front bases in Costa Rica with 156,000 pounds of material and returned north with an unspecified amount of drugs. Gerardo Duran, a veteran Southern Front pilot was later arrested in Costa Rica for the transport of Cocaine to the United States. However, the Contras were not solely responsible for cocaine trafficking on the Southern Front. Witnesses informed Senator Kerry's subcommittee that John Hull, an American rancher residing in Costa Rica worked closely with the CIA and participated in cocaine trafficking activities. Hull played a major role in the Contra supply effort. It was reported on his ranch in Costa Rica that he had six airstrips operating outside the scope of local customs and police. According to Thomas Castillo, the CIA Costa Rican station chief, Hull aided the CIA with military supply between 1984-1986 and at Oliver North's direction, received a stipend of $10,000 per month from a Contra command located in Honduras. Hull's actions came into scrutiny as drugs for guns flights to the U.S. finally caught up with him when his activities prompted an investigation by the U.S. attorney for the Southern District of Florida. As an associate, Gary Betzner who was a veteran drug pilot for Jorge Morales spurred curiosity as rumors arose that he landed at a field in Lakeland, Florida from Hull's ranch in Costa Rica without any search nor entry into customs. This prompted U.S. attorney Jeffrey Feldman along with two FBI agents to come to Costa Rica with the intent of investigating Hull's activities. U.S. Ambassador Lewis Tambs and CIA station chief Castillo told the investigators that he was working for U.S. interests. This caused Feldman to abort the attempt to interview him and three years later, there was still no indictment from the Justice Department. CIA operations in Central America no doubt diminished the DEA's enforcement efforts in creating a drug free enforcement zone. This conflict between the DEA's drug war and the CIA's Contra war became evident in Honduras which was marked the capital of the "northern front" in the war against Nicaragua's Sandinista government. As the DEA closed its Honduran office in 1983 although Honduras became a major transshipment zone for Colombian cocaine shortly beforehand in 1981, it didn't make sense. When the CIA covert war finally wound down by the late 1980s, the DEA was forced to reopen its Tegucigalpa office in Honduras, the same one it had closed. When asked by a reporter why the DEA closed its Honduran office in 1983 initially just as cocaine flows were compounding drastically in the region with the end destination being the United States, the agent responded "the Pentagon made it clear that we were in the way. They had more important business."[64]

The Medellin cartel's rise coincided with the commencement of the CIA covert war that used Contra guerillas to fight Nicaragua's communist Sandinista government. All major U.S. agencies have been on the record with varying degrees of firmness alleging the Medellin cartel utilized Contra forces to smuggle cocaine into the United States. When Contra forces finally opened camps on Nicaragua's borders in the early 1980s, Honduras and Costa Rica were key transit points for the Medellin cartel's flights north to the United States. It was a prime location as the northern Costa Rica borderlands in the 1970s had been abandoned by the country's police effectively permitting the Medellin aircraft to land there on their flights north. These same areas then became the principal site of the closest connection between the Contras and cocaine. An opening of a Southern Front in Costa Rica under the command of Eden Pastora, an independent and charismatic figure who both the CIA and Contra leadership found troublesome to control further fueled drug trafficking activities. However, the Southern Front under Pastora was hindered by a lack of US military aid and the poverty ridden Southern Front quickly turned to cocaine to finance its operations. Furthermore, by allowing drug pilots to refuel at its camps – the Southern Front effectively subsidized the purchase of arms and supplies. However, after becoming too burdensome and with his refusal to subordinate himself to the Contra command in Honduras – the CIA abruptly disconnected all aid to his forces in 1984.[65]

The omnipotent militarization campaigns that began during the Reagan-Bush drug war era vividly declared in 1982 erected a surge in cocaine production and entrepreneurial and political violence. Production of illicit coca doubled between 1982 and 1986 while it dropped steeply in price as Colombian traffickers overinvested in production to counter the rising threat that U.S. interdiction imposed. This shifted the commodity chains as the mid-1980s route of smuggling cocaine through the Medellin-Miami corridor came to an end, the distribution networks shifted to a Cali cartel-northern Mexican route falling in line with the deleterious impact of drug suppression.[66]

Nearing the end of Senator Kerry's investigation in 1989 the Kerry report and Kerry himself severely criticized the Reagan administration but was unable to provide conclusive proof that top Contra leaders or CIA operatives engaged in narcotics trafficking. He came to the conclusion that the Reagan administration had undercut

law enforcement efforts against the Medellin cartel at a time when it

was manifesting into the most dangerous criminal enterprise in U.S.

history. The report also stated that U.S. officials involved in Central

America failed to address the drug issue due to fear of debilitating the

waging proxy war against Nicaragua.[67]

Costa Rica today – Similarities of the Contra/drug trafficking ring and the new, more vicious drug war lurking at Costa Rica's doorstep

The large middle class of Christians in Costa Rica along with

its democratic welfarism had ceded communist forces from effectively

waging civil war and even taking over the country as had happened in

Costa Rica's neighbors'.[68] The abolishment of its army in 1948 allowed

Costa Rica to funnel money into education, social benefits, and

environmental preservation. But their "pura vida" life style is ill

equipped to battle the ruthless Mexican drug cartels. Especially given

the added fact of the advent and implementation of NAFTA and

globalization – processes of which have more than quadrupled drug

seizures to 1.4 million in 2001 from roughly the 300,000 seizures per

year that occurred prior to this sweeping era of globalization that began in the 1990s but have done little to stop the flow of drugs. Proving just how marginal these figures are.[69] The U.S. is now patrolling Costa Rica's skies and waters and providing it with millions of dollars in training and equipment.[70]

Costa Ricans now carry with them immense fears that their country could become more like Mexico, Guatemala, or Honduras as the unchecked power of drug cartels and criminals have left millions in fear.[71] Furthermore, the iron fist policies and the militarization of the war on drugs on behalf of Costa Rica is now severely impacting the tiny Central American paradise. As of recent in the 2010s-decade, Costa Rica has become a major base for the warehousing and repackaging of drugs from Colombia that are then sent north to Mexico and the United States.[72] Meanwhile, Central American drug trafficking has taken on a new role in trafficking that is not limited with solely overland smuggling. Land-based trafficking is defined into three categories including overland smuggling, littoral maritime trafficking and short-range aerial trafficking. In the case of Costa Rica – overland smuggling operations via these varying methods have been witnessed acutely. Authorities were able to identify a route being used by the Sinaloa cartel that operationalized small quantities of drugs entering

Costa Rica from Panama via the Pan-American Highway. Often – the cocaine would be held for several days in storage facilities before being placed onto other vehicles to be driven across the country on major highways. When closing in on the Nicaraguan border, traffickers avoided the official port of entry and sent shipments into Nicaragua on foot or horseback along a remote part of the border.[73]

In elucidating the growing transnational role of Central America as an international drug trafficking hub, the U.S. unequivocally remains the top destination for South American-produced cocaine and Mexico continues to be the primary transshipment path – but rapid changes are happening in shipment routes in Central America, and these changes have far reaching consequences for nations in the region ill-equipped to combat smugglers and cartels. Due to the increased offensive against air and sea smuggling operations – Mexican drug cartels now rely more heavily on land-based smuggling routes – and this shift has been immense. Less than 1 percent of the 600 to 700 tons of cocaine that departed South America for the United States in 2007 transited through Central America according to a December 2008 report conducted by the U.S. National Drug Intelligence Center. Cocaine for the most part passed through the Caribbean Sea or Pacific Ocean in route to Mexico. Now, land-based shipment of cocaine through Central America has swelled. U.S. Ambassador to Guatemala Stephen McFarland in 2009 estimated that more than 300 to 400 tons of cocaine now passes through Guatemala per year.[74] Furthermore, while significantly lower, Nicaragua, Panama, and Costa Rica have all experienced a rise in homicide rates at an average pace of 5 to 10 percent per year.[75]

The role of Mexican cartels leading to the augmented capacity of Central America to serve as a transnational drug trafficking hub cannot be understated. Mexican cartels played a pivotal role as they sought to establish new land-based smuggling routes through Central America. Small quantities of drugs had always transited through the region. But a mixture of poorly maintained highways, persistent border crossings, dicey security conditions and unpredictable local criminal organizations posed such massive logistical challenges that traffickers opted to send the majority of their shipments via firmly established maritime and airborne methods. Suddenly, a multitude of countries in the region increased the monitoring and interdiction of said shipments. Colombia increased the monitoring of aircraft operating in its airspace. Cocaine via aerial trafficking from Colombia has dropped as much as

90 percent since 2003 according to government estimates. Meanwhile, Mexico implemented new radar systems and reduced the number of airports authorized to receive flights originating in Central and South America. Further aiding the deteriorating situation in Central America is the fact that Maritime trafficking has also suffered immensely due to greater cooperation and information-sharing between Mexico and the United States. The maritime technical intelligence capacity of the United States is far reaching and the US has increased its maritime awareness regarding drug trafficking at sea. Evident by 2008 estimates from the Mexican Navy that showed maritime drug trafficking had decreased over 60 percent the last two years. Therefore, in order to make up for the losses in maritime and aerial trafficking – land-based smuggling routes must be used with ever increasing intensity. But now, not by Colombian cocaine producers or Central American drug gangs – but by the much more omnipotent Mexican DTOs.[76]

No single Mexican cartel maintains a monopoly on land-based drug trafficking in Central America as evident by the reports of arrests and drug seizures in the region. However, the security implications will continue to expound. Although there no significant spikes in drug-related violence in Central America outside of Guatemala, the reasons for this are myopic. Large-scale counternarcotic campaigns in the Central American countries have yet to be launched by most governments in the region. Moreover, the quantity of drugs seized remains low – entailing a lack of reprisal on behalf of Mexican cartels attacks against government officials in any country outside Guatemala – where even the president received death threats and had his office bugged allegedly by drug traffickers. Moreover, bribes rather intimidation continue to reign supreme as it is easy to win over corrupted officials given the economic precariousness many countries in the region face as compared to the Mexican cartels. Evident by the roughly $20 billion controlled by Mexican cartels pertaining to the drug trade while the GDP of Honduras stands at a paltry $12 billion. Finally – currently saving Central American governments from significant spikes in violence is the two-front war Mexican cartels are currently fighting in their patria against both the Mexican government and rival cartels. For as long as the war lasts – cartels will be limited in diverting significant resources distant from their home domain.[77]

In looking ahead – the Merida initiative, the U.S. anti-drug aid program that supplies millions of dollars to Mexico and Central American nations, could cause reprisal from Mexican drug cartels if

Central American governments augment their counter narcotics operations either at the request of the U.S. or for more aid money. This could disrupt smuggling operations enough to cause reprisal. Furthermore, very few cartel operatives and resources are necessary if the Mexican cartels choose to undertake assassination campaigns against high-ranking government officials in the Central American region. In part due to the rampant corruption and poor protective security for political leaders in the region. Cartel experience doing so in Mexico doesn't necessarily hurt either. Finally, as drug traffickers continue to expand operations into Central America – turf battles amongst competing Mexican cartels or between the Mexicans and local criminal organizations could significantly deteriorate the region's security situation.[78]

The ongoing militarization and global police apparatus on the war on drugs and the economics driving it

Efforts at curtailing drug trafficking organizations influence in the region entail in its most recent form developments of U.S. training of foreign police as a network of international law enforcement academies (ILEAs) which are funded primarily through the INL budget. Negotiations for an ILEA for Latin America commenced in

Costa Rica in 2004. ILEAs intents are to encourage strong partnerships among regional countries seeking to address common problems revolving around criminal activity along with the added purpose of developing a vast network of alumni who will exchange information with their U.S. counterparts to assist in transnational investigations. The primary purpose of ILEA in Latin America is counter drug in nature. However, ILEA-South is controversial as members of the Costa Rican Congress permitted a proposal increasing national and civil society input into the governance of the academy to make explicit the nonmilitary nature and goals of training conducted there. It remains an issue of high sensitivity to Costa Rica given that it abolished its military and maintains a constitutionally mandated stance of neutrality. The U.S. embassy advised the Costa Rican government in March 2004 that proposed changes to the agreement were unacceptable, especially those that revolved around the ban on military training.[79]

It's important to understand the economics of the drug trade too in order to paint a picture of why actors delve into this illicit enterprise. In examining the wholesale value of cocaine along the Pacific coast between Colombia and the United States – a fresh kilo of cocaine runs approximately US$1000 on the Caribbean Coast of

Colombia. Its price rises sharply in value passing along Panama, Costa
Rica, Nicaragua, Honduras, reaching about US$13,000 in Guatemala.
Once the product reaches the United States, its value increases to over
US$30,000 wholesale and more than US$170,000 on the retail market.[80]
With these substantial monetary figures, it's no wonder Central
America is becoming a transnational drug trafficking hub and
distribution center. As long as the lucrative economics of the drug trade
endure, the global policing and militarization of the war on drugs will
endure also.

Some somber thoughts

History is repeating itself. Just as Colombian traffickers
utilized Costa Rica as a staging and refueling area during the Contra
war, Costa Rica has reemerged as a central theatre in the war on drugs
and the global commodification of this lucrative enterprise. Moreover,
an operational presence of la Familia Michoacán, the Sinaloa Cartel,
Gulf Cartel, and even the vicious Los Zetas cartel have all been
reported. Costa Rica's growing role in the political economy of the
drug trade has led to the rapid rise of local drug markets, criminal
organizations and crimes from homicide to simple burglary.[81] As a
result of the militarization of the war on drugs, Costa Rica's prison

population increased over 50 percent between 2006 and 2012. It now has the third-highest incarceration rate in Central America. Lower than only El Salvador and Panama and many of those jailed in the fight against drugs are being held for minor crimes.[82]

Above all else, the onset of the Cold War in 1948 until its conclusion in 1990, the US secured the overthrow of at least 24 governments in Latin America through military forces, CIA revolts and assassinations, and the encouragement of local military and political forces to intervene without direct US participation. As a consequence, Latin Americans were ruled by governments more conservative and reliably more anti-communist than Latin American voters would have otherwise chose. Moreover, between 1975 and 1991 – the death toll throughout the Central American region stood at nearly 300,000 in a population of less than 30 million while more than 1 million refugees fled the region.[83] Costa Rica, as demonstrated, played a critical role. And the repercussions are still being felt well into the 21st century.

Notes

---

[1] Steven Bishop, *A Historical Study of The Effectiveness of US Security Assistance to Panama, Costa Rica and Nicaragua* (Air Force Inst Of Tech Wright-Patterson Afb Oh School of Systems and Logistics, 1986), 56-57.
[2] Ibid., 62-63.
[3] Ibid., 63.
[4] Ibid., 63-64.
[5] Ibid., 69-70.
[6] Ibid., 71-73.
[7] Ibid., 73-75.
[8] Ibid., 75.
[9] Ibid., 63-64.
[10] Bishop, "A Historical Study of The Effectiveness of US Security

Assistance to Panama, Costa Rica and Nicaragua," 45.

[11] John Coatsworth, *The Cold War in Central America, 1975–1991* (Cambridge: Cambridge University Press, 2010), 211.

[12] Bishop, "A Historical Study of The Effectiveness of US Security Assistance to Panama, Costa Rica and Nicaragua," 50.
[13] Ibid., 51.

[14] *Chronology: Nicaragua: The Making of U.S. Policy, 1978-1990.* 116.

[15] Bishop, "A Historical Study of The Effectiveness of US Security Assistance to Panama, Costa Rica and Nicaragua," 2.
[16] Ibid., 3.
[17] Ibid., 5.
[18] Coatsworth, "The Cold War in Central America," 201.
[19] Hey Jeanne, Lynn Kuzma. *Anti-U.S. Foreign Policy of Dependent States: Mexican And Costa Rican Participation in Central American Peace Plans,* (Comparative Political Studies, 1993), 31.
[20] Ibid., 34-35.
[21] Ibid., 35.
[22] Ibid., 36.
[23] Bishop, "A Historical Study of The Effectiveness of US Security Assistance to Panama, Costa Rica and Nicaragua," 42.
[24] Ibid., 44.
[25] Jeanne, Kuzma, "Anti-U.S. Foreign Policy of Dependent States: Mexican and Costa Rican Participation in Central American Peace Plans," 36-37.

[26] Ibid., 37.
[27] Bishop, "A Historical Study of The Effectiveness of US Security Assistance to Panama, Costa Rica and Nicaragua," 8.

[28] Jeanne, Kuzma, "Anti-U.S. Foreign Policy of Dependent States: Mexican and Costa Rican Participation in Central American Peace Plans," 37.

[29] Ibid., 58.

[30] Ibid., 37-38.
[31] Sabine Kurtenbach, *Why Is Liberal Peacebuilding So Difficult? Some Lessons from Central America,* (European Review of Latin America And Caribbean Studies, 2010), 95.
[32] Michael Klare. *Subterranean Alliances: America's Global Proxy Network,* (Journal of International Affairs, 1999), 98.
[33] Ibid., 99.
[34] Kurtenbach, "Why Is Liberal Peacebuilding So Difficult? Some Lessons from Central America," 101.
[35] Jeanne, Kuzma, "Anti-U.S. Foreign Policy of Dependent States: Mexican and Costa Rican Participation in Central American Peace Plans," 40.

[36] Ibid., 41.
[37] Bishop, "A Historical Study of The Effectiveness of US Security Assistance to Panama, Costa Rica and Nicaragua," 94.
[38] Ibid., 94.
[39] Ibid., 95-96.
[40] Ibid., 97.
[41] Ibid., 97.
[42] Ibid., 65.

[43] Graeme Mount, *Costa Rica and the Cold War, 1948-1990*, (Canadian Journal of History, 2015), 313.

[44] Jeanne, Kuzma, "Anti-U.S. Foreign Policy of Dependent States: Mexican and Costa Rican Participation in Central American Peace Plans," 41.

[45] Bishop, "A Historical Study of The Effectiveness of US Security Assistance to Panama, Costa Rica and Nicaragua," 101.
[46] Jeanne, Kuzma, "Anti-U.S. Foreign Policy of Dependent States: Mexican and Costa Rican Participation in Central American Peace Plans," 42.

[47] Ibid., 45.
[48] Amin Azki, *"Communism – Central America." Tri – State Defender*, (1986), 1.

[49] Mark Phythian, *The Illicit Arms Trade: Cold War and Post-Cold*

*War, (*Crime, Law and Social Change, 200), 13.

[50] Ibid., 13

[51] Peter Kassebaum, "Structural Model of The Fuerza Publica (Costa Rican Police)." (1989), 3

[52] Phythian, "The Illicit Arms Trade: Cold War and Post-Cold War," 14-15.

[53] Peter Kassebaum, "Structural Model of The Fuerza Publica (Costa Rican Police)." (1989), 4.

[54] Phythian, "The Illicit Arms Trade: Cold War and Post-Cold War," 14-15.

[55] Moisés Naim, *Illicit* (Anchor Books, 2005), 75

[56] Phythian, "The Illicit Arms Trade: Cold War and Post-Cold War," 14-15.

[57] Peter Kassebaum, "Structural Model of The Fuerza Publica (Costa Rican Police)." (1989). 4

[58] Naim, "Illicit," 75

[59] John Galvin, *Peacetime Conflict: Realities of War* (United States Southern Command Apo Miami 34003, 1986), 12.

[60] Phythian, "The Illicit Arms Trade: Cold War and Post-Cold War," 14-15.

[61] Jeanne, Kuzma, "Anti-U.S. Foreign Policy of Dependent States: Mexican and Costa Rican Participation in Central American Peace Plans," 47-48.

[62] Kurtenbach, "Why Is Liberal Peacebuilding So Difficult? Some Lessons from Central America," 99.

[63] Jeanne, Kuzma, "Anti-U.S. Foreign Policy of Dependent States: Mexican and Costa Rican Participation in Central American Peace Plans," 44.

[64] Alfred McCoy, *The Politics of Heroin: CIA Complicity in The Global Drug Trade* (Lawrence Hill Books, 2003), 490-492.

[65] McCoy, "The Politics of Heroin: CIA Complicity in The Global Drug Trade," 488-489.

[66] Paul Gootenberg, *Andean Cocaine: The Making of a Global Drug* (The University Of North Carolina Press, 2008), 313.

[67] William Marcy, *The Politics of Cocaine* (Lawrence Hill Books, 2010), 112.

[68] Amin Azki, *"Communism – Central America." Tri – State Defender*, (1986), 2.
[69] Naim, "Illicit," 77.
[70] Michael Weissenstein, *"Tourists Paradise of Costa Rica Toughens Its Stance with Us Backing in War Against Drugs; Costa Rica Toughens Stance in US-Backed Drug Fight",* (The Canadian Press, 2013), 1.
[71] Ibid., 1.
[72] Weissenstein, "Tourists Paradise of Costa Rica Toughens Its Stance with Us Backing in War Against Drugs; Costa Rica Toughens Stance in US-Backed Drug Fight," 1.
[73] Stephen Meiners, *Central America: An Emerging Role in The Drug Trade* (Stratfor, 2009) 2.
[74] Ibid., 1.
[75] Gabriel Demombynes, *Drug Trafficking and Violence in Central America And Beyond* (World Bank, 2011), 0.

[76] Meiners, "Central America: An Emerging Role in The Drug Trade," 1-2.
[77] Ibid., 3-4.
[78] Ibid., 4.
[79] Coletta Youngers, Eileen Rosin, Eileen *Drugs and Democracy in Latin America* (Lynne Rienner Publishers, Inc, 2005), 81-82.

[80] Demombynes, "Drug Trafficking and Violence in Central America And Beyond," 9.

[81] Weissenstein, "Tourists Paradise of Costa Rica Toughens Its Stance with US Backing in War Against Drugs; Costa Rica Toughens Stance

in US-Backed Drug Fight," 2.

82 Ibid.,3.
83 Coatsworth, "The Cold War in Central America," 221.

Bibliography

"Chronology: Nicaragua: The Making of U.S. Policy, 1978-1990".
    DNSA Collection: Nicaragua, 1-139.

Alfred McCoy, *The Politics of Heroin: CIA Complicity in The Global
    Drug Trade*. (United States of America: Lawrence Hill Books,
    2003), 1-710.

Azki, Amin. "Communism – Central America." Tri – State Defender,

March 29, 1986.

Bishop, Steven. "A Historical Study of The Effectiveness of Us Security Assistance to Panama, Costa Rica and Nicaragua. No. Afit/Glm/Lsy/86s-5." *Air Force Inst Of Tech Wright-Patterson Afb Oh School of Systems and Logistics*, (1986): 1-114.

Coatsworth, John. "The Cold War in Central America 1975–1991." *Cambridge University Press* no.3 (2009): 201-221.

Coletta Youngers and Eileen Rosin, *Drugs and Democracy in Latin America.* (United States of America: Lynne Rienner Publishers, Inc, 2005), 1-415.

Demombynes, Gabriel. "Drug Trafficking and Violence in Central America And Beyond." *World Bank* (2011): 1-23.

Galvin, John. "Peacetime Conflict: Realities of War." *United States Southern Command Apo Miami 34003*, (1986): 1-22.

Hey, Jeanne A.K and Lynn M. Kuzma. "Anti-U.S. Foreign Policy of Dependent States: Mexican And Costa Rican Participation in Central American Peace Plans." *Comparative Political Studies* 26 no.1 (1993): 30–62.

Kassebaum, Peter. "Structural Model of The Fuerza Publica (Costa Rican Police)." (1989): 1-8.

Klare, Michael. "Subterranean Alliances: America's Global Proxy Network." *Journal of International Affairs* 43 no.1 (1999): 97-118.

Kurtenbach, Sabine. "Why Is Liberal Peacebuilding So Difficult? Some Lessons from Central America." *European Review Of Latin American And Caribbean Studies / Revista Europea De Estudios Latinoamericanos Y Del Caribe* 88 (2010): 95-110.

Moisés Naim, *Illicit.* (United States of America: Anchor Books, 2005),

1-340.

Mount, Graeme. "Costa Rica and The Cold War 1948-1990." *Canadian Journal of History* 50 no.2 (2015): 290-316.

Paul Gootenberg, *Andean Cocaine: The Making of a Global Drug.* (United States of America: The University Of North Carolina Press, 2008), 1-442.

Phythian, Mark. "The Illicit Arms Trade: Cold War and Post-Cold War." *Crime, Law and Social Change* 33 no.1 (2000): 1-52.

Weissenstein, Michael. "Tourists Paradise of Costa Rica Toughens Its Stance with US Backing in War Against Drugs; Costa Rica Toughens Stance in Us-Backed Drug Fight." The Canadian Press, February 18, 2013.

William Marcy, *The Politics of Cocaine.* (United States of America: Lawrence Hill Books, 2010), 1-356.

Made in the USA
Middletown, DE
23 October 2023

41322958R00033